University of Montana

Report of the President

University of Montana

Report of the President

ISBN/EAN: 9783743337886

Manufactured in Europe, USA, Canada, Australia, Japa

Cover: Foto ©ninafisch / pixelio.de

Manufactured and distributed by brebook publishing software
(www.brebook.com)

University of Montana

Report of the President

UNIVERSITY OF MONTANA

PRESIDENT'S REPORT

FOR THE FIVE MONTHS ENDING NOV. 30, 1895.

HELENA, MONTANA
STATE PUB. CO., STATE PRINTERS AND BINDERS
1895

THE MONTANA STATE BOARD OF EDUCATION.

EX-OFFICIO.
GOVERNOR J. E. RICKARDS, President.
                    H. J. HASKELL, Attorney General.
  E. A. STEERE, Supt. Public Instruction, Secretary.

APPOINTED.
R. G. YOUNG, Helena . . . . Term Expires February 1st, 1899
O. F. GODDARD, Billings . . .   "   "   "   "   1899
JAMES REID, Bozeman . . .   "   "   "   "   1896
A. H. WETHEY, Butte . . . .   "   "   "   "   1896
J. E. MORSE, Dillon . . . . .   "   "   "   "   1897
T. E. COLLINS, Great Falls . .   "   "   "   "   1897
J. M. HAMILTON, Missoula . .   "   "   "   "   1898
H. H. GRANT, Grantsdale . .   "   "   "   "   1898
CAMERON C. WYLIE, Helena . . . . Clerk of the Board

EXECUTIVE COMMITTEE OF THE STATE UNIVERSITY.
J. H. T. RYMAN, President . . . . Missoula
T. C. MARSHALL . . . . Missoula
HIRAM KNOWLES . . . . Missoula

THE FACULTY.

OSCAR J. CRAIG, A. M. Ph. D., President.
Professor of History and Literature.

S. A. MERRITT, B. S.
Professor of Natural Science.

MISS CYNTHIA ELIZABETH REILEY, B. S.
Professor of Mathematics.

W. M. ABER, A. B.
Professor of Latin and Greek.

FRED C. SCHEUCH, M. E., A. C.
Professor of Modern Languages and Temporarily in charge of the Department of Applied Science.

MARY OLIVE GRAY,
Instructor in Music.

MARY A. CRAIG, B. S.
Librarian.

PRESIDENT'S REPORT.

UNIVERSITY OF MONTANA,
MISSOULA, MONTANA, NOV. 30, 1895.

To the State Board of Education,
Helena, Montana:

GENTLEMEN:—In accordance with Section 5 of the "act to establish, locate, maintain and govern the University of the State of Montana," the following report for the year ending November 30, 1895, is respectfully submitted.

On July 5, 1895, five days after my term of service began a preliminary circular was issued in which the general plan of the organization of the University and of its work was given to the public.

The following extracts from this circular relate to Buildings and Grounds, Courses of Study, Preparatory Department, and Tuition, Fees and School Terms.

"BUILDINGS AND GROUNDS."

"A commodious and well-arranged building is being fitted up for university purposes and will be ready for occupancy before the beginning of the college year. This building will contain lecture rooms, laboratories, library and reading room, and assembly room."

"The building is heated by steam and will be lighted throughout by electricity. It is located on the south side of the Missoula river and is easily reached, as there are good sidewalks extending to the university and the street cars pass within two squares of the grounds."

"Courses of Study."

"Courses of study will be arranged in Ancient and Modern Languages, History, Philosophy and Literature, Mathematics, Chemistry, Physics, Biology, and some of the Applied Sciences."

"Preparatory Department."

"A two years' course of preparatory work will be provided. This work will be so arranged that it will not only furnish the necessary preparation for the Freshman class of the University, but will also give a course of instruction adapted to the needs of those who wish to prepare themselves for teaching. A special announcement containing course of study will be issued soon."

"Tuition, Fees, and School Semesters."

"By legislative enactment tuition is free to all students who have been residents of the State of Montana for one year next preceding their admission to the University, except in certain departments not yet established and for extra studies."

"A matriculation fee of ten dollars will be charged and is payable one-half in advance at the beginning of each semester."

"The year will be divided into two semesters of nineteen weeks each. The first semester will begin September 11, 1895, and the second February 3d, 1896. The Christmas holidays will be from December 21, 1895, to January 6th, 1896, inclusive."

The first of August a more complete announcement was sent out containing the Course of Study, the Plan of Work, a description of Laboratory Facilities and some other items of interest.

The Course of Study as printed in the announcement has been put in operation and is as follows:

COLLEGIATE COURSES OF STUDY.

Beginning with the college year of 1895-6, the University will offer the following courses of instruction:—

    A.—A Classical course, leading to the Degree of A. B.
    B.—A Philosophical course, leading to the Degree of B. Ph.
    C.—A General Science course, leading to the Degree of B.S.
    D.—A Course in Applied Science which will ultimately be developed into different courses, leading to their respective degrees in the Industrial Arts.

The work of the year will be divided into two equal Semesters. For convenience in classification, the work of each department of study will be divided into courses and fractional courses. One course shall mean the equivalent of one hour's lecture or recitation five times a week for one semester. Two hours of laboratory work will count the same as one of lecture or of recitation. In the absence of any definite statement, the Faculty reserves the right to prescribe the order in which the different courses shall be taken. Twenty-six full courses as here defined are required for graduation in any of the departments of the University.

Admission to Collegiate Departments.

Candidates for admission to any of the collegiate Departments of the University must be at least sixteen years old and present satisfactory evidence of good moral character.

Those who have been members of other Colleges and Universities must bring certificates of honorable dismissal.

For admission to the Classical Course, leading to the degree of A. B., the applicant must present the equivalent of the following courses found in the Preparatory Department. (See page 20.)

    Mathematics—Courses 1, 2, 3 and 4.
    Latin—Courses 1, 2, 3 and 4.
    Greek—Courses 1 and 2.
    English—Courses 1, 2, 3 and 4.
    Science—Courses 1, 2, 3 and 4.
    History and Civics—Courses 1 and 2.

For admission to the Philosophical Course, leading to the degree of B. Ph., there is the same requirements as for the Classical Course except that courses 1 and 2 in German are taken in the place of Greek.

For admission to the General Science course, leading to the degree of B. S., the following courses or their equivalents are required.

    Mathematics—Courses 1, 2, 3 and 4.
    Latin—Courses 1, 2, 3 and 4.
    English—Courses 1, 2, 3 and 4.
    Science—Courses 1, 2, 3 and 4 with additional laboratory work in Physics.
    Drawing—Courses 1 and 2.
    History and Civics—Courses 1 and 2.

For admission to the course in Applied Science.

    Mathematics—Courses 1, 2, 3 and 4.
    English—Courses 1, 2, 3 and 4.
    History and Civics—Courses 1 and 2.
    Drawing Courses 1 and 2.

COLLEGIATE DEPARTMENTS OF INSTRUCTION.

COURSES OF STUDY IN THE DEPARTMENT OF HISTORY LITERATURE, AND PHILOSOPHY.

History.

(3 times per week.)

1. Ancient and Mediaeval History.
2. Modern European History.
3. The History of England and the English Constitution.
4. American History with especial reference to the development of Political, Social, and Industrial Institutions.

Literature.

(3 times per week.)

1. Rhetoric—Exercises in Writing, Criticism of Themes.
2. Rhetoric—Lectures and Recitations. Theme writing and criticism continued as in course 1.
3. English Literature—Lectures, Readings from representative Authors. Text-book: Minto's Manual of English Prose.
4. Theme study of some typical selections from Chaucer, Shakespeare, Browning, and Emerson.

Philosophy.

(3 times per week.)

1. The Elements of Psychology—Especial prominence will be given to the practical phases of the subject as relates to Mind culture.
2. Ethics—Lectures and Recitations. An attempt will be made to apply the scientific method to the investigation of the right in human conduct and individual relation.

Political Economy.

(3 times per week.)

1. The Elements of Political Economy—The subject will be treated from the historical standpoint.

COURSES IN SCIENCE.

Physics.

(1st Semester.)

1. General Lectures—Mechanics, Heat, Electricity, Magnetism, Acoustics, and Optics. Recitations and Laboratory Work.
2. Continuation of Course 1.

These two courses will be required of all students in the University Department. The work in Physics of the Preparatory Department will be similar to the above courses, but more elementary.

3. A Course in Laboratory Practice—The Theory and Methods of Physical Measurements. Must be preceded by Course 1. The equivalent of Stewart & Gee, Vol. 1.
4. Electricity and Magnetism—Measurements and Application to the Industries. Continued during 2d Semester as an elective.
5. Mathematical Physics—Fundamental Equations of Theoretical Physics. Mathematical theory of sound, light, and electricity.

Courses 3, 4 and 5 may be elected by students in the general science course in place of equivalent work in the biological sciences.

Courses 1 to 4 inclusive are required of students in the course in Applied Science.

Chemistry.

Course 1.—Descriptive Inorganic Chemistry; Lectures, Text Book and Laboratory Work. (Required as a preparatory study for students in the Applied Science course.)

Course 2.—Qual. Analysis, Lectures on Elementary Organic Chemistry with Laboratory Work.

Courses 1 and 2 will be required of all students in the college department.

Course 3.—Advanced Inorganic Chemistry, Preparation of Commercial Compounds, etc., Organic Chemistry, Preparation and Study of Organic Compounds. Must be preceded by courses 1 and 2.

4. Quantitative Analysis—Volumetric and Gravimetric and applications to the analysis of ores, crude metals, slags and technical products.

5. Course 4 continued to include blowpipe analysis and assaying. Must be preceded by Courses 1 and 2.

Courses 3, 4 and 5 may be elected by students in the General Science course in place of equivalent biological work.

MINERALOGY.

1. Lectures and Recitations—Characteristics of the different minerals, determinative mineralogy, the application of chemical tests, of blowpipe analysis, laboratory work, required of students in the General Science course, and elective in place of equivalent technical work in the Applied Science course.

GEOLOGY.

Course 1. Physiographic, Lithological, and Dynamical Geology —Lectures and recitations, identification of rocks.

2. Historical Geology—The succession of the rocks of the globe, the records they contain as to the successive conditions of the earth, the changes in its oceans, continents, climate, life. Must be preceded by a course in Botany and Zoology.

3. Economic Geology—A consideration of the topics usually classified under this subject.

BIOLOGY.

1. General Biology—Introductory to Botany, Zoology, and advanced Physiology. Lectures and laboratory work. Required as a preliminary to all advanced work in this department.

2. Course in Botany, should be preceded by course in General Biology—Anatomy and histology of plants, the elements of vegetable physiology, and the principles of morphology and classification. Special attention to the flora of the region.

3. Physiology—Must be preceded by Courses 1 and 2 in Physics and by course in General Chemistry.

4. Animal Histology—Open to those taking Course 3.

5. Zoology, Invertebrate—A general course in the morphology and classification of Invertebrates. For illustrative material in this department the University has secured a collection of sea Invertebrates from the National Museum.

6. Vertebrate Zoology—Accompanied by dissections of typical vertebrates. Invertebrate Zoology will also be taught by dissections and laboratory work so far as material can be had.

THE DEPARTMENT OF MATHEMATICS.

THE FOLLOWING COURSES HAVE BEEN PROVIDED.

1. A course in Plane Geometry.
   First Semester 5 times per week.
2. Solid and Spherical Geometry.
   Second Semester 5 times per week.
3. Plane and Spherical Trigonometry.
   First Semester 5 times per week.
4. Higher Algebra.
   Second Semester 5 times per week.
5. Analytical Geometry.
   See page —.
6. Differential and Integral Calculus.

Students in all courses will take 1, 2, 3 and 4. Courses 5 and 6 are optional except to those taking the course in Applied Science, in which case both are required subjects.

THE DEPARTMENT OF LATIN AND GREEK.

GENERAL INFORMATION:
  1. In Latin, the Roman pronunciation will be used.
  2. The writing of Latin and Greek will be practiced throughout Courses 1, 2, 3, 4.
  3. There will be almost daily practice in reading and translating at sight.

COURSES IN LATIN.

1. VERGIL'S AENEID—First three books, elements of prosody.
   4 periods.
2. VERGIL'S AENEID—Books IV., V. and VI.
   4 periods.
3. HORACE—First half, selected odes.
   4 periods.

CICERO—Second half, one essay, one or two orations, selected letters.
4 periods.

4. LIVY AND TACITUS—Selections.
4 periods.

5. HORACE—First half, selected Satires and Epistles.
4 periods.

PLAUTUS AND TERENCE—Second half, one play from each.
4 periods.

6. Private Life of the Romans. Descriptive, no knowledge of Latin required for this course.
3 periods.

7. Rapid Reading Course, Catullus, Horace, Pliny's Letters.
8. Rapid Reading Course in Latin Dramatic Literature.

COURSES IN GREEK.

1. XENOPHON'S ANABASIS—Three books.
4 periods.

2. HOMER'S ILIAD—Two books.
4 periods.

3. HOMER CONTINUED—Selections from the Iliad and the Odyssey.
4 periods.

4. GREEK HISTORIANS—Fernald's Selections or a similar work
4 periods.

5. PLATO—Selections.
4 periods.

6. GREEK DRAMATISTS—One play each from Aeschylus, Sophocles, and Euripides, selections from Aristophanes.
4 periods.

7. Private Life of the Greeks. Descriptive, no knowledge of Greek required for this course.
3 periods.

8. Demosthenes' Orations.

DEPARTMENT OF MODERN LANGUAGES.

German.

Two years work has been arranged in German. The first year is devoted to the study of grammar.

> Course 1 and 2 (19 weeks each 5 hours a week.) Joyne's-Meissner, German Grammar, Joyne's-German Reader.

In the second year, a select course of reading is followed with exercises in composition and conversation.

> Course 3 and 4 (19 weeks each 5 hours a week.)
> Reading, composition, and conversation.
> SELECTION OF CLASSICS—Harris' German Composition, White's German Prose, Goethe's "Iphigenia," "Hermann und Dorothea." "Maria Stuart," "Wilhelm Tell" or "Die Jungfrau von Orleans."
> SELECTION OF MODERN PROSE.—"Aus dem Staate Friedrichs des Grossen." "Jensen Die Braune Erica." "Undine."

French.

Two years are given to the study of French. The first year is devoted to a study of grammar.

> Courses 1 and 2 (19 weeks each, 5 hours a week.)
> GRAMMAR AND READERS.—Edgreen's Grammar, Histoires Novelles, Super's Reader, Souvestre's "Confessions d'un Ouvrier," Sandeau's "Mademoiselle de Seigiliere."

In the 2d year, the course consists of readings and translations of various selections from classical and modern writers with a study of syntax, idioms, etc., and with exercises in composition and coversation. Essays in French are required.

> Courses 3 and 4 (19 weeks each, 5 hours a week.)

THE DEPARTMENT OF APPLIED SCIENCE.

Chemistry.

Courses I., II., III., IV., V. But students may elect equivalent work in other departments of Applied Science in place of courses III., IV. and V.

Physics.

Courses I., II., III., IV. Course V. elective, but necessary for some courses in Applied Science.

Mineralogy I.

Geology. Courses I., II. Course III. will be required of some students, depending upon selection made in other courses.

Descriptive Geometry.

1. Nineteen weeks, 2 hours per week.
Methods of representing geometrical magnitudes by drawing.

Analytical Geometry.

1. Nineteen weeks, 3 hours per week.
Text: Wentworth's Analytical Geometry.

Plane Surveying.

1. Nineteen weeks, 2 hours per week.

Shop Work.

Technical Instruction—Four courses, 19 weeks 5 hours a week.
Course 1.
(a) Recitations on the cutting edges of wood; the care and adjustment of wood working tools; the shrinkage and warping of woods; the form, adaptation, and strength of joints.
Goss' Bench Work in Wood.
(b) Lectures on wood working machines and pattern making, molding, and casting.
Course 2.
Exercises in planing, sawing, splicing, dovetailing, and other work involving the use of carpenter tools.

Mechanical Drawing.

Four courses, 19 weeks, 5 hours a week.
Course 1 and 2.—
(a) Drawings from copy of the details of machines.

(b) Drawings for built-up pulley patterns, pipe bends, etc.
(c) Free hand drawings with dimensions of details of machines.
(d) Lettering.

Courses 3 and 4.
(a) Drawings from scale from parts of actual machines.
(b) Ink shading and tinting. The representation of flat and curved surfaces by ink tints and of engineering materials by colors.

Graduation and Degrees.

While it is hardly expected that all of the work offered will be called for in the current year of 1895-6, still the amount of work required for graduation in the different courses is stated in order to present the plan of organization.

In order to secure the recommendation of the faculty for graduation from the University in any of the respective lines of work that have been outlined, it will be necessary that the student complete the equivalent of twenty-six full courses as already defined in the section concerning collegiate courses.

That the needs and special inclinations of the different students may be consulted as far as possible, certain of these courses are required for each of the respective degrees and the rest are left for the students' selection.

The following is a statement of the amount of required work for the different degrees and the number of elective courses allowed.

For the Degree of A. B.

In Latin, 1, 2, 3, 4, 5, 6	4 3-5	full courses
" Greek, 1, 2, 3, 4, 5, 6, 7	5 2-5	" "
" Mathematics, 1, 2, 3, 4	4	" "
" History, 1, 2	1 1-5	" "
" English and Literature, 1, 2, 3, 4	2 2-5	" "
" Political Economy, 1	3-5	" "
" Psychology and Ethics, 1, 2	1	" "
" Physics, 1, 2	1 1-5	" "
" Chemistry, 1	4-5	" "
Electives	4 4-5	" "
Total	26	" "

For the Degree of B. Ph.

In Latin, 1, 2, 3, 6	3	full courses
" Greek, 7, Descriptive course	3-5	" "
" German, 3, 4	2	" "
" History, 1, 2	1 1-5	" "
" Literature, 1, 2, 3, 4	2 2-5	" "
" Political Economy, 1	3-5	" "
" Psychology and Ethics	1	" "
" Physics, 1, 2	1 1-5	" "
" Chemistry, 1	4-5	" "
" Biology, 1, 2	2	" "
" Mathematics, 1, 2, 3, 4	4	" "
Electives	7 1-5	" "
Total	26	" "

For the Degree of B. S.

In Latin, 1, 2	1 3-5	full courses
" Mathematics, 1, 2, 3, 4	4	" "
" German, 1, 2, 3, 4	4	" "
" History, 1, 2	1 1-5	" "
" Literature, 1, 2, 3, 4	2 2-5	" "
" Political Economy, 1	3-5	" "
" Psychology and Ethics, 1 and 2	1	" "
" Chemistry, 1, 2	1 3-5	" "
" Physics, 1, 2	1 1-5	" "
" Biology, 1, 2	2	" "
" Geology, 1	1	" "
" Mineralogy	3-5	" "
Electives	4 4-5	" "
Total	26	" "

In the Course in Applied Science no degrees have been arranged, for the reason that the equipment of this Department is not yet complete, and full lines of work can not be given at present.

THE PREPARATORY DEPARTMENT.

It is supposed that the average student will complete the work of the Preparatory Department in two years, if due diligence is employed. The arrangement of semesters and courses is just the same as in the college, except that there are no electives. Each collegiate course has its appropriate preparatory work.

COURSES OF INSTRUCTION.

MATHEMATICS.

5 periods a week.

1. ARITHMETIC. With special attention to Fractions, Percentage, Proportion and the Metric System of Weights and Measures. First Semester.
2. ELEMENTARY ALGEBRA. Second Semester.
3. Algebra continued. First Semester.
4. Plane Geometry. Second Semester.

SCIENCE.

2½ periods a week.

1. Physiology.
2. Physical Geography.
3. Physics.
4. Physics.

ENGLISH.

5 periods a week.

1. English Grammar Reviewed.
2. Grammar and Composition.
3. Rhetoric. Elements of.
4. American Literature.

LATIN.

5 periods per week.

1. A first Latin book: elements of grammar; selections read from Gradatim or a similar book.
2. Selections from Latin reader continued; Cæsar's Gallic War, second book; sight reading; writing Latin.

3. Cæsar's Gallic War continued, about four books read; sight reading; writing Latin.
4. Cicero's orations and letters, three orations and some letters; sight reading; writing Latin.

GREEK.

5 periods per week.

1. A first Greek book; elements of grammar; selections from Xenophon's Anabasis or the New Testament; writing Greek; sight reading.
2. First book of the Anabasis: sight reading; writing Greek.

HISTORY.

2½ periods a week.

1. U. S. History.
2. Civics of the U. S. and of Montana.

FREE HAND DRAWING.

Two courses; 19 weeks, 5 hours per week.
Course 1.
Principles of free hand drawing. (A) From geometric solids. (a) In outline. (b) In washes of water color. (c) In charcoal.
(B) (a) Groups of common objects, as books, vases, chairs, tables etc. (b) Casts of ornament. (c) Interior, as corner of a room.
Course 2.
Design for capital, panel, etc., and original design for surface, decoration in color.
Shaded study from antique figure.

MODERN LANGUAGE.

1. GERMAN. See Course 1, Collegiate Department.
2. GERMAN. See Course 2, Collegiate Department.

ADMISSION TO THE PREPARATORY.

Applicants for admission to the Preparatory Department should be at least fourteen years old, and well grounded in the elements of an English education. They must be able to pass a creditable examination in the elements of Arithmetic, Elementary Grammar, Geography, Reading, and Spelling.

The following circular was issued concerning the Department of Music:

THE UNIVERSITY OF MONTANA.

Department of Music.

The Department of Music in the University of Montana, will be under the direction of Miss Mary Olive Gray, graduate of the New England Conservatory of Music, Boston, Massachusetts.

Instruction may be had in piano forte, voice building, harmony, theory and ensemble playing. For further information in regard to tuition, length of term and rent of instruments, address, or apply in person to Miss Gray, at the University.

Registration in the Department of Music as well as in all other Departments of the University will begin Wednesday, September 11, 1895.

For information in regard to the University, its facilities, courses of study, etc., address

OSCAR J. CRAIG,

Missoula, Montana   President.

The President and Board of Trustees,

Invite you to attend the

Opening of The University of Montana.

Missoula, September 11, 1895.

Exercises at 3:30 p. m.

OPENING EXERCISES

OF THE

University of Montana

Music	Mandolin, Banjo and Guitar Club
Invocation	Rev. C. H. Lindley
Music......Spinning Song—*Litolff*	Miss Mary Olive Gray
Address	Lieut. Gov. A. C. Botkin
Music	Mandolin, Banjo and Guitar Club
Address	Judge Hiram Knowles
Music..Sonate Pathetique, op 13-*Beethoven*	Miss Mary O. Gray
President's Address	Oscar J. Craig
Music	Mandolin, Banjo and Guitar Club

BENEDICTION.

Missoula, Mont., 3:30 p. m. Sept. 11, 1895.

The University was formally opened on September 11, 1895. The exercises were held in the assembly room and were attended by a large number of people. Many came from distant parts of the State to show their interest in the cause of education and to take part in the exercises.

The invitations issued and the programme of exercises will be found on preceding pages of this report,

The addresses of Lieut. Governor A. C. Botkin, Judge Hiram Knowles, Senator Thomas H. Carter, Senator Wilbur F. Sanders, President James Reid of the Agricultural College and President Oscar J. Craig will be found in the appendix to this report.

EQUIPMENT OF THE UNIVERSITY.

University Grounds.

The University Grounds comprising forty acres of excellent land are on the south side of the Missoula river just where it leaves Hell Gate canon to enter the beautiful Missoula valley. The outlook is to the west, the mountain slope being in the rear. In the foreground and to the right lying on both sides of the river in the city of Missoula, but the view extends uninterrupted for many miles down the valley. On the left is the Bitter Root valley with Mt. Lo Lo in the distance. On the right and beyond the river Mt. Jumbo and the canon of the Rattlesnake. This river affords the waterworks with an unlimited supply of water remarkable for its purity and cleanness.

Arrangements have been made by citizens of Missoula, for fencing the grounds, supplying them with water and planting shade trees without expense to the State, and this will be done as early in the spring of 1896, as possible.

January 14, 1895, the citizens of school district No. 1, Missoula County voted $3,000.00 (special tax) for the purpose of completing the south side school building, which when completed was to be tendered to the State Board of Education for the free use of the State University for a period of two years or until a University Building could be constructed.

Thereafter the School Trustees contracted for the completion of the building which contract included certain tables, cases, etc., of the estimated value of $800.00. The total cost to the district was $3,754.00.

The South Side building as it stood had cost a little over $15,000 by the giving up of this building for University purpose the Board was obliged to provide other accommodations for the public schools at a cost of $700.

Buildings.

The University Building is located in South Missoula and is easy of access from all parts of the city as there are excellent sidewalks and the street car line has been extended to the University Grounds.

The building is a modern brick structure containing three stories and a basement.

The first floor contains the lecture rooms in Mathematics, Greek and Latin, Modern Languages, History and Literature, and the President's office. These lecture rooms are fitted with excellent desks and supplied with blackboards, maps, charts and other illustrative material.

On the second floor is found the Library, Chemical Laboratory, Physical Laboratory, and Biological Laboratory. The equipment of these is given in another place.

The third floor is the Assembly room. This has a seating capacity of about 300 and is provided with rostrum, chairs, piano and individual desks enough to accommodate the present attendance of students.

The heating apparatus, lavatories and lunch rooms are in the basement. After taking the room necessary for the accommodation of these there is left a floor space of 24 ft. by 52 ft. which is being fitted up for a laboratory for shop practice in bench work in wood, wood turning, pattern making, etc. The tables for Mechanical Drawing have been placed temporarily in the lecture room of the Department of Modern languages.

The Library.

This is a well lighted room situated on the second floor and is provided with cases for books and periodicals, and newspaper rack.

There are at present in the library 817 volumes exclusive of pamphlets and periodicals. So far the library contains but little except that material most needed for reference in the work already in progress in the University. This list for the most part includes Dictionaries, Encyclopedias, Histories, standard works in Literature, Science, Politics, Philosophy and Economics.

The following periodicals are on file:

    The Forum.
    The Popular Science Monthly.
    Harper's Weekly.
    Harper's Monthly Magazine.
    The North American Review.
    The Atlantic Monthly.
    The Cosmopolitan.
    Montana Educator.
    The Scientific American.
    Political Science Quarterly.
    Ladies' Home Journal.
    American Journal of Psychology.
    The Rockies.
    The Independent.
    The Dial.
    The Century Magazine.
    Review of Reviews.
    Scribner's Magazine.
    The Chautauquan.

The following Newspapers are on file and are for the most part donated by their respective publishers.

  The Daily Missoulian, Missoula.
  The Bitter Root Times, Hamilton.
  The Anaconda Standard, Anaconda.
  The Western News, Hamilton.
  The Montanian, Thompson Falls.
  The Evening Republican, Missoula.
  The Troy Times, West Troy.
  The Plainsman, Plains.
  Montana Silverite, Missoula.
  Flathead Herald-Journal, Kalispell.
  The Columbian, Columbia Falls.
  Helena Independent, Helena.
  The Citizens Call, Philipsburg.
  The Montana Mining Area.
  The Darby Sentinel.

Large additions ought to be made to the library equipment as soon as possible, or the work will be retarded for lack of proper material for the use of both Faculty and students.

Department of Chemistry.

One laboratory is given to this subject. Its arrangement is the usual one which obtains for work in general descriptive chemistry. There are 24 working places for students, and reagent bottles for 12 students. The department is provided with Hoskins' Assay furnace, crucible furnace No. 4 and No. 3 muffle, and the six gallon gasoline tank. Also one general analytical balance by Becker, with agate planes, and sensitive to .1 mg. Also an assay balance by the same makers sensitive to 1-50 mg. There are also other pieces of quantitative apparatus, such as burettes, pipettes and a few graduated vessels. The Dangler burners are used as the general source of heat in the Chemical Laboratory, and while they are an excellent substitute for gas, their range of usefulness, however, in many directions is limited. Adjoining the Chemical Laboratory is a store

.room which is being used to a considerable extent as a quantitative laboratory.

The amount and variety of work called for in the department of Chemistry is more than was anticipated. The department has been called upon to do a good deal of quantitative work from the first, inthe way of general assaying. We have been called upon also to make some water analyses. We believe general determinations of various kinds to be a part of the legitimate work of the Chemical Department of the State University, and earnestly recommend that as soon as practicable this department be more completely equipped for the work of quantitative analysis, much of which will be called for by students in the regular work of the University before the end of the year.

DEPARTMENT OF PHYSICS.

The equipment in this department, while, of course, a modest one, has been much appreciated. Besides many other pieces of apparatus with which this department is supplied, we note especially the apparatus for the subjects of light and electricity. The University has the best projection apparatus with accessories, manufactured in America and it is not surpassed by the best European makers. This projection apparatus consists of a Stereopticon by J. B. Colt & Co. of N. Y., with microscope, polariscope and vertlcal attachments, also attachments for projecting the spectrum. This stereopticon can be converted, at a moment's notice into a calcium light, sunlight, or electric light apparatus. With it we are able to throw upon a screen ordinary lantern transparencies, anything which the ordinary powers of the microscope can reveal, galvanometer deflec-·tions, and other physical apparatus, and also all ordinary chemical reactions. Other accessories in our possession, such as Nichol prisms, tourmaline plates, glass tank with graduated arc, for refraction and total reflection, achromatic prisms, etc., in connection with the projection apparatus above described, enable us to demonstrate the successive steps in the development of the undulatory theory of light.

In electricity and magnetism, besides many minor pieces of apparatus, the equipment in this department contains sóme very good testing and measuring instruments:—namely, astatic galvanometer and thermo-pyle, for the detection of very slight variations in temperature. This galvanometer is wound with one coil of low, and one coil of high resistance, and as it is also differential it therefore, admits of a wide range of work in measuring resistance and electromotive force of circuits. There is also a sine and tangent galvanometer with sliding compass box, manufactured by Queen & Co. This is a standard instrument, and it is also wound with coils of high and low resistance. Also a reflecting galvanometer, with lamp and reading scale. Also we have one dead-beat and balistic galvanometer, not affected by the proximity of masses of iron. Besides these galvanometers we have a standard Wheatstone bridge and resistance box, correct to 1-5 per cent, a standard slide-wire-meter bridge, and Clark's standard cells, and also shunts for galvanometers.

Besides the above necessary testing, and measuring instruments, we are supplied with a Wheatstone bridge and resistance set of simpler construction for students just beginning work in electrical measurement.

In magnetism we are supplied with large diamagnetic apparatus, dipping needle, electrometer and magnetometer, and various other smaller pieces of apparatus. For frictional electricity we are supplied with an excellent 26-inch Tcopler Holtz machine.

Our equipment also includes one of E. S. Ritchie's best automatic value air pumps. This pump has stood the test in the laboratory of the University of producing a vacuum represented by a barometric difference of only 1 millimeter.

An Atwood machine for determining the laws of accelerated motion has been supplied for this department, also specific gravity balances after Jolly and Mohr.

There are 35 students now receiving instruction in Physics. The work thus far has been by study of text-book and recitations. The text-book is supplemented by laboratory work done by the student himself. The number of students in this department is much greater than was anticipated, and the laboratory conveniences are inadequate, even for the present number of students. Apparatus for physical measurements in other departments of this subject, besides electricity will be a necessity in the near future, as well as more room.

BIOLOGICAL LABORATORY.

This department has, besides the usual equipment of dissecting tables, etc., some very excellent microscopes obtained from Leitz of Wetzlar, Germany. One of these stands is the best made by these well known makers, and it has the following accessories:—three eye pieces, a series of five objectives, one being a one-twelfth oil emersion. It has also a revolving stage, with substage condenser after Abbe, and the Iris diaphragm. It has eye and stage micrometers, and accessory Nichol prisms for polarization, and also a camera lucida after Abbe.

Besides the above described microscope this laboratory is also provided with the large dissecting microscope after the same makers, and also two student's microscopes with rack and pinion and micrometer adjustments, two eye pieces and three objectives each. There is also in this department a camera for photo-micrography, a complete set of staining fluids, glass slips and covers, a student's microtome after Bausch and Lomp, Anthony's copying reducing, and enlarging camera, with accessories for making lantern transparencies. For the purpose of physiology this department has been supplied with an articulated skeleton, and as we are in possession of material for mounting microscopic slides, these slides can be prepared from time to time; a few have already been added to the equipment of this department.

For purposes of illustration in Botany about five hundred botanical specimens have been contributed to this department, nearly all being representative of the flora of Montana. These specimens, however, need mounting to permit of their being more conveniently filed in botanical cases, and for this purpose mounting material is much needed. This material should be obtained from dealers who make a specialty of such articles.

Consistent with the suggestion of Supt. Hamilton of the State Board of Education, and with the recommendation of the Board, application was made to the Secretary of the National Museum at Washington for duplicate specimens of minerals. Sea invertebrates, fishes and plants. Up to this time this department has received from the National Museum ninety-nine land and water invertebrates, one hundred and five fishes, both salt and fresh water specimens. The above are nearly all alcohol specimens.

Besides the above gift there was also donated by the National Museum to the museum of the University a set of ninety-eight rock and mineral specimens.

The museum is receiving almost daily additions in way of mineral specmens principally from Montana, and some from other portions of the country.

It is most earnestly requested that all who are interested in the University, and especially in the preservation of valuable material for scientific work, should take special pains to contribute to this department. Time and circumstances are fatal to nearly all specimens, but being properly cared for and placed in the museum of the University they would be preserved to the benefit of the coming generations.

The Cobban Collection.

In connection with this department should be noted also the very fine mineral collection of Mr. Robert M. Cobban which this gentleman has kindly placed in the museum for the use of the University.

This collection is a very valuable one especially in the matter of the variety of representative minerals which it contains, and will be of great service to the University in Mineralogy.

Mounted Specimens.

The University is also indebted to Mr. Charles Emsley of Missoula, for the beginning of a collection of mounted specimens.

DEPARTMENT OF APPLIED SCIENCE.

Course of Study and Equipment.

Students upon entrance into the Freshman class in the course of Applied Science are required to pass an examination in:

Mathematics as laid out in Courses 1, 2, 3 and 4.
English as laid out in Courses 1, 2, 3 and 4.
History and Civics as laid out in Courses 1 and 2.
Drawing as laid out in Courses 1 and 2.

This department has for its object the giving of a good general education making a specialty of those technical branches belonging to Engineering, also to furnish a systematic and progressive education in the use of tools, machinery and materials, combined with as much theoretical instruction as will furnish a thorough knowledge of the principles involved. For those students not having a sufficient preparation, the preparatory course is provided as shown in the above schedule.

DRAWING.

The course in drawing commences in the Preparatory year and continues throughout the college course. Instruction in Free Hand Drawing is given in the Preparatory year. It includes drawing from copy and model perspective drawing from objects and free hand sketches of machinery. These sketches will be used for instrumental drawing later in the course. The work in the Freshman and Sophomore years consists of drawing from copies and models and practice in drawing sections of various parts of machines such as screw-threads, etc.

In the Junior year drawings for use in the pattern shop will be required; consisting of free hand sketches of machinery, which will be drawn to scale in the drawing room making a full working drawing that can be used in the shops.

In the Senior year the work required will be the designing of engines and machinery, the students original idea in the building of special machinery will then be brought out. Lettering symbolic hatching, line shading, tinting, tracing and blue printing receives attention during the course.

There have been provided for the use of students in Mechanical Drawing, six drawing tables. These accommodate two students each, and each contain four drawers provided with lock and key so that the student can leave his drawing materials in the table. Each table holds two drawing boards 36x25 inches.

SHOP WORK.

Shop practice begins in the second term of the Freshman year. During the first term lectures in wood working machinery are given. Goss' Bench Work in Wood is used as a text to familiarize the student with the uses and the care of carpenter's tools. During the second semester the knowledge thus gained is put to practice in the wood working shop.

The course in the Wood Shop will consist of exercises, such as sawing, planing, joining, splicing, mortising, dovetailing, framing and paneling. All the operations of carpentry are thus taught. These exercises are followed by those in turning, the course as laid out will begin in the 1st semester of the Sophomore year, and will consist of exercises in turning of wood, such as cylinders, beads, cups to a given size. Exercises which involve the use of chucks and face plates. When the student has completed this course in turning, he will take up pattern making, molding and casting, the drawings for this having been made in the drawing room by the students. Lectures in pattern making, moulding and casting will be given during the 2d semester of the Freshman year. The 2d semester of the Sophomore will be taken up in bench work or vise work in iron such as filing, chipping, key fitting, etc., both in iron and steel; after these exercises machine work will be taken up such as turning screw threads of certain pitch, turning cylinders, boring, planing and the common exercises in this line of work. Students will be required to forge their own tools, grind them and keep them in good order. The work in iron and steel will not be given this year as the shops for this work will not be in readiness during this college year.

RECITATIONS.

During the Freshman year the purely technical work which will be given besides their required work will be:
    Lectures in Bench Work in Wood.
    Lectures in pattern making, moulding and casting.
    In Sophomore year: Heat (Garnet's.)
                      Steam boilers (Text: Wilson and Flather.)
    In Junior year: "Valves and Links."
                   Graphical Statics.
                   Transmission of Power.

In the Senior year: Elements of Mechanics.
                      Strength of Materials.

Students in the Applied Science course are required to take the full course in Mathematics consisting of Plane and Solid Geometry, Plane and Spherical Trigonometry, Higher Algebra, Analytical Geometry, Descriptive Geometry, Differential and Integral Calculus.

Wood Shop.

A part of the basement of the University building will be used for this purpose. It is well lighted and ventilated and contains 24 ft. by 52 ft. of floor space. It affords room for eight benches arranged for two students to work at each bench. Each bench will be supplied with two sets of tools.

Each set of tools contains:

- (1) 6" square, try and mitre combined.
- (1) 8" bevel, (sliding.)
- (2) 8" marking gauges.
- (1) Scriber.
  Firmer chisels (8 in the set.)
  Gauges (4 in the set.)
- (1) 22" cross-cutting saw.
- (1) 24" ripping saw.
- (1) 8" drawing knife.
- (1) Fore plane.
- (1) Jack plane.
- (1) Smooth plane.
- (1) Set of auger bits.
- (1) Bit brace.
- (1) Set of brad awls.
- (1) Carpenters hammer.
- (1) Mallet.
- (1) Nail set.

These are kept in lockers, each student having one set which he is to care for and use. Besides these the shop contains the following tools which are for general use.

1 Framing square.
1 Beading plane.
1 Mitre box.
1 Matching plane.
1 Wood plow.
1 Grindstone and several oil stones.

Every available inch of space in the University building being already in use, Messrs. Northquist and Jackson of the Missoula Iron Works, have tendered to the University the use of their Foundry and Machine works for instructional purposes.

Having the use of their excellent equipment of machinery and other necessary appliances, the department will at once be able to put in operation its entire course of work including the molding, the casting and the machine work in iron and steel.

ATTENDANCE.

The total number of students matriculated is 118. The following table shows the subjects in which instruction has been given and the number of students studying each subject.

Number in	Chemistry classes	7
"	" Physics "	35
"	" Physiology "	40
"	" Latin "	87
"	" Greek "	3
"	" German "	14
"	" French "	19
"	" Mechanical Drawing	9
"	" Wood Work	9
"	" Shop Practice	9
"	" Geometry classes	8
"	" Algebra "	43
"	" Arithmetic "	46
"	" History "	59
"	" Rhetoric and Literature	37
"	" English Grammar and Composition	50
"	" Music	11

APPENDIX.

APPENDIX

ADDRESS

OF

LIEUT. GOV. A. C. BOTKIN.

Considerations of a character so entirely personal that they need not be mentioned would have led me to decline your courteous invitation if the occasion had been any other than that in which we are here permitted to participate. But my estimate of this event appeals more forcibly to my interest and my sympathy than any other in our history, and I cannot comprehend how any citizen of Montana should fail to appreciate its momentous and prophetic character.

Among the suggestions of which this scene is so richly fertile is a reminiscence that may be briefly recited. About forty years ago with twenty pupils assembled in a small brick house that had been erected for the public schools of Madison, with a faculty consisting of two professors and a tutor, the University of Wisconsin had its modest inception.

For some years as a student and later as an alumnus I have watched the growth of that institution. It had its "day of small things." Its fund was scant; its constituency was a people environed by the hard conditions of what was then a frontier; the state not only withheld its aid, but actually made a charge for administering the endowment from the general government and sectarians or those who were striving to maintain colleges of their own denomination, looked upon it with a more or less jealous eye.

From the small beginnings which I have inadequately pictured the University of Wisconsin has grown to splendid proportions. It occupies buildings the cost of which may be estimated at two million dollars; its observatory contains some of the finest astronomical instruments that can be found in the world; its equipment in all departments of natural science is unsurpassed; under the presidency of C. K. Adams, formerly president of Cornell, and one of the most enlightened and progressive educators of his time, it has a faculty of thirty professors and instructors; its average attendance of pupils exceeds two thousand, and its motto, "Numen Lumen," has justified itself and sheds its beams afar.

I mention this in part for the encouragement of the people of Missoula with the assurance that there are many within the sound of my voice who will live to witness a like growth from the seed which their far-sighted liberality has enabled the state to plant to-day; but surely the forecast ought to be no less gratifying to all the people of Montana.

There is a reminder in what I have been saying of an interesting subject for reflection; and I now refer to the action and reaction between the older colleges of the east and those state universities of the west that have been built up with the aid of grants from the United States. It was almost always inevitably true in the early histories of the latter they drew upon the former for their instructors, and that these brought with them, and in a measure impressed upon the new institutions the characteristics and traditions of their elders. This was a service of no inconsiderable value, especially in that it aided to erect and maintain high standards and to guard them against the danger of becoming diploma shops where degrees were dispensed below any just cause of mental effort or discipline.

But it soon appeared that the influence was to be mutual. Yale, Harvard and Princeton for example were what might be called an aristocracy of learning. They were quite self complacent, and assuming the perfection, each of its own methods, for a premise naturally they could see no excuse or occasion for introducing changes or permitting anything to jar them out of their well worn grooves. Having their own governing bodies with substantially perpetual succession they offered scant hospitality to suggestions of innovation.

The State Universities of Michigan, Wisconsin and Minnesota, using these institutions as illustrations grew up under far different conditions Necessarily they felt in a less degree the constrictive pressure of tradition. Then they were in closer touch with the people and their government was more responsive to the tendencies and impulses or progress. So they came to recognize that a young man might be a well rounded scholar even though he were a little uncertain in the conjugation of the second aorist passive in Greek verbs ending in *mu iota*. Gradually they introduced elective courses of study; they bestowed more attention on modern languages aud literature, and, most notably and most wisely they increased the facilities for instruction in those physical sciences that afford the most interesting and profitable field for investigation.

These innovations proved to be popular because they were progressive and answered to the sentiment that called for ampler recognition of the utilitarian principle in education. The older colleges of the east soon found themselves confronted by this dilemma. They must either conform themselves to the requirements of what is sometimes called "the new learning" or lose their patronage. They chose the former alternative and reconstructed their courses of study upon broad and liberal lines; but the fact is the most prominent one in the history of modern education that this great reformation had its source in State Universities, such as that which we are assembled to dedicate.

I have spoken of the utilitarian principle in education, and it is upon this subject that my particular purpose is to utter a word of warning. The tendency of the period is toward the hastiest results. At this remote time disclaiming the culture of the Greeks as unworthy of our attention, we yet adopt the precept of Sophocles:

"To kosmion metheisa, sun tachei molein."

Or to put it in the language of a great American of the period, "Speed is at once the great virtue and the great vice of our generation. We demand that morning glories and century plants shall submit to the same conditions and flower with equal frequency."

We live in an age of labor-saving. The inventive genius of mankind has supplied machines by which that which was before the labor of a day is now the work of an hour. Our civilization has sought; and not without a large measure of success, to annihilate time and space. The grasp and utilization of the forces of nature which is the distinctive achievement of the present age has reduced to realities that which were before the wildest imaginings of the dreamer and the fairy fantasies of the poet have come to be the commonplaces of our daily observance.

The consequences of this tendency are easily conceivable. There is fever in the blood and fire in the brain. There is a frantic impatience for results, and this feeling has naturally invaded the domain of education. There has grown up the conviction that for the acquisition of comprehensive symmetrical development of the faculties of the mind there can be substituted specialized training that will prepare each individual for the particular pursuit that he has projected for himself. There is no greater and there can be no more mischievous fallacy, and this occasion would be wasted if no voice were raised in protest against it.

The question that we have to answer is: How can a young man or young woman be best fitted for the duties and enjoyments, the larger results of life? We will be answered that a knowledge of Latin and Greek cannot contribute to this end, but this conclusion is not to be hastily conceded. In those tongues are enshrined the sources of our language, our literature, our jurisprudence, our social and political systems and all the constituent elements of our civilization, and surely that time is not to be counted as lost which is expended in drinking at the fountain head from which flows this Pactolian stream. In philosophy, art, culture and most of that which contributes to the graces and amenities of human life, the Greeks, having reference to their conditions and their time are unsurpassed by any race that ever lived upon the globe; while a system of laws that survives in substance throughout Europe and America, and some of the richest treasures of literature and the ripest products of human thought emanate from that marvelous city that

> "Sat upon her seven hills,
> And from that throne of beauty ruled the world."

But here we may invoke, and not reject the principle of utilitarianism. The French philosopher uttered a great and pregnant truth when he said: "Words are things." Language is an instrument common to all the pursuits of life; and I submit with the solemnity of deep conviction that there can be no more valuable acquisition for man or woman—protesting that I mean no sarcasm as to the latter than the possession of an abundant vocabulary, and facility and precision in its use.

The statement may be confidently added that the best means that has been found for the attainment of this result is the study of the classics. Omitting other considerations, observe how largely we draw upon the Greek and Latin languages, from time to time, as occasion demands, for the enrichment of our own verbal stores. The nomenclature of science is almost wholly derived from the Greek; that language alone possesses the wealth and a certain quality difficult to define that fit it to fill the requisitions of scientific progress. Inventive genius devised an instrument that transmits the human voice over vast distances of space, and we wanted a name for it: the dead Greeks, across vast distances of time, responded by "telephone." There has come into popular use a vehicle consisting chiefly of two wheels, and to supply the need of something by which to designate it, from the same gifted race we acquired by annexation the word "bicycle."

The Latin language enters very largely into the web and woof of the English that we use in ordinary conversation, and it may be urged with undeniable force that a knowledge of its vocabulary and structure is indispensable to the thorough and scientific mastery of our own tongue.

But I must not further expand this part of my theme. The pupils of the University of Montana will not be required to study Latin or Greek. Without either, they will find ample occupation in the pursuit of profitable and delightful studies, and will be eligible to receive its degrees. I do not overlook the immense advantages of the modern languages, nor is it with any desire to influence the judgment of parent or pupil in this respect that I have uttered protest against the more or less prevalent disposition to relegate Greek and Latin to the limbo of the past with alchemy and astrology, and to condemn them as unworthy of any place in modern education.

In the curriculum of our university a prominent place will no doubt be assigned to mathematics and as to this department of learning it need only be said that it has been for untold ages one of the largest contributors to the advancement of the human race, and is to-day essentially associated with employments that occupy the chief place in the welfare of mankind. There is no study that is so conductive to the development of the reasoning faculty; and it is a fact of some significance that Alexander Hamilton made it his invariable custom in preparation for the argument of a law suit to read a problem of euclid.

But I do not feel called upon to pass in review all the different branches in which this university will afford instruction. The tendency of modern institutions of learning to give larger attention to the natural sciences will be fully represented. From the information which I have respecting the apparatus and equipment which have already been provided for instruction in this class of studies, I am able to say that they surpass anything which had been secured by the University of Wisconsin when it had attained the age of ten years. There can be no question but this was a wise expenditure, and with the aid of the zealous and scholarly instructor who has been assigned to this chair results may be expected that will be of estimable value not alone to pupils, but also to the discovery and development of the resources of the state.

In what I have said my purpose has been to advocate the claims of a liberal education as opposed to specialized training alone. In brief the university of to-day is not to be confounded with the scholasticism of the middle ages that assumed to teach, for example, the science of "angeldogy," and devoted precious time to disputations on the question whether an angel could be transferred from one point to another without moving through the intervening space. The collegiate course as it now exists is the well ripened product of the experience learning and humanity of all ages brought forward to the living present. Shall we willingly exchange its approved advantages for such instruction as is imparted by the business college or the technical school? The one invokes and insures the healthful and symmetrical development of all the faculties of the mind; the other is necessarily and confessedly partial and one sided.

I wish that my voice might reach all the parents of Montana in an appeal to consider seriously the question whether they desire that their children shall confront the duties and responsibilities of life equipped with a well grounded and well rounded scholarship, or be cast upon the world, like England's deformed monarch, "scarce half made up."

Prof. Huxley once said that it was the business of the state to provide a ladder reaching from the gutter to the university upon which every child should have the chance of climbing as far up as he was fit to go. With the event that will make this day forever memorable, Montana has measurably performed this duty, but not wholly. We cannot claim this without further legislation, first in the direction of appropriations as liberal as our revenues will permit, and secondly, to bring different educational institutions into systematic and harmonious co-ordination to the end especially that every high school in the state shall become a feeder of the University of Montana. So shall there go forth from this institution an ever-growing band of young men and women, enlightened, loyal, progressive and richly endowed with all the Christian graces, before whose coming ignorance, bigotry and political corruption shall flit away like sombre shades at the approach of light and paeans of joy and thanksgiving shall ascend in glad chorus to the bright arch of Montana's sky.

ADDRESS

OF

JUDGE HIRAM KNOWLES.

"Ladies and Gentlemen, Students of the University of Montana—I was selected as a member of what has been termed the local board of the State Board of Education. I have taken some interest in the starting into active operation of this University of Montana. While my heart has been in the work, I do not think I have actually labored as extensively as some of my associates in this good cause. It may be for this reason that I have been called upon to say a word on this occasion. The national government recognizing that education was the corner stone of our republican edifice, that without education our republican institutions must perish, contemplated the establishment of such an institution as this, and granted to the state large tracts of land for its maintenance. The legislature of the state, in its wisdom saw fit to establish this university at this place. The citizens of Missoula exercised considerable influence in securing this result. They felt that here in our fertile valley, surrounded by grand and picturesque mountains, was a fitting location in which to plant the state's chief institution of learning.

"Considering to-day the condition it presents, I cannot but believe the selection was a proper and fortunate one. There were other thriving and industrious communities who were desirous that this coveted prize should fall to their portion. No one can blame them for having labored for the realization of this cherished hope. I do not believe, however, that any of them could offer the inducements here afforded—inducements presented by nature itself. The elevation here is such as to insure a healthy atmosphere and yet not so high as to generate nervous disorders or to occasion excessive labor to the heart in performing its functions. The climate is more mild than in many portions of Montana. The soil is fertile, the grand mountains in this portion of our state covered by thick and almost untraversed forests, more attractive than the Black Forests of Germany, invite the enterprising and daring youth of our state to investigation and exploration. The sparkling and limpid waters in our mountain streams are attractive to the eye and give music to the listening ear. The university campus in time will be covered by arching elms and maples and graceful poplars and made as attractive as the surroundings of a Harvard, a Yale or a Princeton.

"We are molded and influenced by every environment. Scenes of beauty and grandeur cultivate the love of the beautiful and sublime in our nature. Mountain lands have been loved the best by our race. Here amid these scenes the ingenious and spirited youth of Montana will learn to love their state; patriotism will become as natural to them as to the Switzers reared among the fastnesses of the Alps. In coming years, wherever they may roam, their hearts will turn affectionately to surroundings here presented. They will find but few sections of country that surpasses it in scenic attractions. While the people of Missoula wished the establishment of this university in their midst, they no less ardently welcomed the opening to-day of its doors to the students of Montana and the commencement of that high educational instruction which will prove its worth and ability to bless our mountain State. This is an important day for our community. We will always revert to it, I trust, with pride and satisfaction.

Other communities may have much to offer for the good and honor of our common state, but this university shall be our offering. The achievements of our hands crumble to dust and pass away, while the achievements of intellect become immortal. The temple of the Hebrews ornamenting their chief city among the hills of Palestine no longer gladdens the eye, but the wisdom of Solomon is still cherished and the songs of David read and sung. The temples and monuments erected in ancient Greece lay in sad ruins, but the immortal poems of Homer are still read, the elevated philosophy and teachings of Socrates are still prized and studied, and the profound contemplations of Plato are the property of our learned and curious and still to-day exercise a wide and enduring influence. The Coliseum is a ruin and the palaces of the Cæsars are no more, but the odes of Horace, the histories of Cæsar and the orations of Cicero are read with pleasure and profit by the scholar and the aspiring student of our land. Ancient Rome and her institutions perished beneath the heel of the unlettered barbarian, but the laws promulgated by her praetors and expounded by her lawyers have enriched the modern jurisprudence of every civilized land.

"Who can estimate the benefit conferred upon modern society by the university of Paris or the colleges of Oxford and Cambridge of England. At a time when ignorance was the rule, when the nobility of Europe were in ignorance of many facts that are common knowledge to the most of our school children, and could not write their names and give authenticity and validity to the documents to which they were parties only by their seals, these institutions created a thirst for knowledge. The enthusiasm that accompanied the instructions of an Abelard of Paris, cannot be appreciated in our time. We can state with assurance that these institutions were most potent factors in creating that intellectual advancement which has enabled the nations of Europe as well as the United States to call themselves the civilized nations of the world. It is difficult to state what mighty influence for good Harvard university, Yale, Princeton and Williams and many colleges have had upon the intellectual condition of the nation. They kept burning on this side of the Atlantic the intellectual lights of Europe. The two Americans who did the most to instigate our declaration of independence were alumni of American colleges. Adams was a graduate of Harvard university and Jefferson of Williams and Mary's college of Virginia.

"Since the time of our colonial life, what a long list of colleges have been added to these which existed in the days of our dependence, institutions which have created and inspired our intellectual life. To-day we add another to the list—the University of Montana. To-day it becomes a living potent force in intellectual life. As I scan its curriculum of study, I see set down the ancient and modern languages, language the garments in which thought clothes itself, the implements of ideas forged in the white heat of necessity and which enable them to become living and potential factors in the contests of the world; mathematics which enables us to measure the distance to the sun and the fixed stars, and to weigh them in balances; English literature, that which shows the evolution of our race and gives sweetness to our intellectual life. The natural sciences, here can be learned, the processes and forces by which God works in this planet of ours. Such a course of study If well pursued cannot but be of benefit and must meet with approval. What in education is here accomplished shall be for the benefit of humanity. The thought of the learned in ancient times was that the discoveries of science should not be for the use of man, that this would be a bare use. A learned Grecian apologized for having used his knowledge in physics in the service of his country. His excuse was that it had been used in war, which was a noble art. The modern thought is the Baconian one, that all knowledge must be valued for its utility to humanity. By this university humanity is to be benefited.

"On this important day for our mountain-girded community, Missoula extends a welcome hand to those who have come here as instructors in this university and to the strangers within our gates who have come to witness its opening, and in the language of Tiny Tim, we would say 'God bless you, every one, and may his blessings rest upon the work of this hour.' To-day the Montana University becomes a living, potent factor in the educational life of this State. All Montana should consider with interest and approval the work now being inaugurated for her, and now is started an intellectual life which shall do it honor and will last when her proudest and most enduring edifices shall have crumbled into ruins."

ADDRESS

OF

SENATOR WILBUR F. SANDERS.

Mr. Chairman, Mr. President, Professors, Tutors and Scholars, Ladies and Gentlemen:—

I count it an unalloyed felicity that the unfailing hospitality of the presiding officer identifies my name with a most significant event in the history of the State of Montana. Having been a witness of every great occurrence which has signalized her career, I could not forbear being a silent witness of those ceremonies by which she consecrates and dedicates this generously endowed and most highly prized of all her civic Institutions to Learning, for the security of the present and the renown of the future. In the vicissitudes of things, some occasions rise above the sordid and common place, as peaks of sunken continents cleave oceans' waves and pierce the arching sky, to be observed forever from near and from far. Unless I mistake me in the perspective, we are the witnesses of such an occasion now and here. An event of such transcendent dignity may not be fitly served by extemporaneous speech, which is all I am permitted to give. The orators and scholars in the august presence of her pioneers and principal officers have responded to your eager solicitudes and expectations with high and fitting words, and speech and silence here alike conspire to give promise that this chosen abode of Learning, crowned with the benedictions and endowed with the generous largess of the noble Commonwealth shall henceforth from generation to generation and from century to century enjoy every felicity, and from hence like,

"Another morn risen on mid noon"

shed that refulgent light which "was never yet on sea or land."

How proudly contrasts this meeting of scholars and the disciples of Learning, with that noisy and vulgar show, which, with puerile and discordant voices, profanes the ambient air. The age is sordid and the era chaotic in its devotion to sordid themes. Into the temples of Learning, into our sacred places, into our holy of holies where angels walk reverently uncovered and unshod, with brazen and stolid front bursts our degraded and modern millionaire as if the Divine effulgence opened its gateways only to golden keys. Audaciously and impudently they assume to dictate what shall be taught, and command that omniscience shall speak only with "'bated breath and whispering humbleness." Far from this presence be ye profane!

We hear from time to time belittling and apologetic speech for Learning and weak enticements held forth that it is the pathway to money-getting and place, and what the world names success in life; and this method of speech is sought to be reinforced by identification with a great name, the founder and father of inductive philosophy.

Bacon strove to awaken a zeal for Learning among peoples slowly emerging from that pathetic and melancholy midnight known as the Dark Ages, which, objectively considered is the solecism of human history, and what wonder if in his yearnings and beseechings, his wide scope of vision comprehended other forms of utility than Nobleness and Beauty, and that by all that was true and commanding, on their level, he beckoned them to "come up higher." But whosoever is familiar with "The Advancement of

Learning," and his other works will well certify that this mean and sordid view can find no refuge in his illustrous name. "Learning," he says, "endueth men's minds with a true sense of the frailty of their persons, the casualty of their fortunes, and the dignity of their soul and vocations, that it is impossible for them to esteem that any greatness of their own fortune can be a true or worthy end of their own being and ordainment."

Another and a greater philosopher has said "Get wisdom and with all thy getting, get understanding. Take fast hold of instruction, let her not go, keep her for she is thy life," from which the deduction is as easy as it is true that the totally ignorant man, in that inner and truer vision, is dead already.

Learning lifts men from their dead selves to higher things, sets every occurrence of life in orderly array. and gives to its devotees companionship of the stars. It refines, purifies and solidifies human character, and leaves

"—— all meaner things"
To low ambition and the pride of Kings."

It is not the tide waiter of greed, it cannot be the portico of the temple of Mammon.

For the love of Learning here let it be pursued as a bride, with an intensity of devotion which no coarse ambition shall invade. Hold not before these pupils hopes of money or office. Be it not theirs to project ambitions on selfish lines. Be it rather their high purpose to save the world from shame and thrall,

"Clothing the palpable and familiar
With golden exhalations of the dawn."

Another fallacy of confusion deforms some modern speech, that education is a good thing, that Learning is to be desired, but it is essential, that in addition there must be the accompaniment of morality, of virtue. As if morality and virtue were a thing apart from Learning, as if it were an affirmative something to accompany or be separated from Learning at the behest of some teacher or pupil. The rounded sphere of Learning comprehends the essence of human integrity, of virtue, of morality, which inseparably pervades it as an atmosphere, certifying to its genuineness and setting upon it a Royal Seal. Nay, scholars, I cannot consent that wickedness or wrong can find refuge or hiding place in or around or behind real and genuine Learning. Find for them, I pray you, some other more fitting name. Let us conform to the properties of speech and the facts of morals and metaphysics, and call them Ignorance.

Learning will be taxed to its utmost in solving the problems which are now imminent. Ominous portents becloud our social and economic sky. Elemental axioms are challenged, and empiricism and charlatanism prescribe nostrums with a confidence born of ignorance and the cherished treasures of civilization are made the football of blind leaders of the blind. Only in the secure refuge of the Divine Philosophy shall the great Republic hold her secure joyful way.

So on this goodly day, auspicious in achievement and hope, let us highly resolve that hence shall go forth civic pride and just views of life and duty; that here the youth of Montana shall be fitted and inspired for deeds of high emprise; that here all Learning shall have her abode, draped in robes of enticing beauty; and that from influences here generated, the noble State shall rest in more secure confidence upon the valorous devotion of her daughters and sons. Here let Learning be adored and commended. Here let Truth, whose inspiring ways are pleasant, give confidence to her devotees and surround us all with the benedictions of the blest.

And mindful of the solicitudes which this hour from the remotest hamlet in the Commonwealth in patriotic intensity converge on these ceremonies; let this Institution inculcate love of Country. May the Institutions of Liberty repose securely upon all who shall go forth from these halls equipped for duty in the battle which is before. Let not the spirit of provincialism dwarf it; but may it be as cosmopolitan as the expanded sky. May we here encourage and commend the audacious courage of Learning. Let nothing in upper or nether world claim immunity from her interrogation and judgment. Her place in the Divine economy will not be occupied until to her every knee shall bow. Above all, and beyond all, teach her disciples to have the courage and confidence of their convictions, speaking them boldly, without dissimulation or prevarication in the face of day.

Mr. President and Ladies and Gentlemen of the Faculty of the University of Montana; the State confers upon you a high responsibility and a most solemn duty.

In the pivotal crisis of their history, she confides to you her most precious possessions, and largely in your hands are our affections, our destinies and our hopes. May our young men when they shall go forth from these classic halls with the approval and seal of this most cherished Institution, be indeed true Knights of Learning, filled with lofty aim, fitly reciting the proud boast of Sir Gallahad in Tennyson's immortal poem:

> "My good blade carves the casques of men,
> My tough lance thrusteth sure.
> My strength is as the strength of ten
> Because my heart is pure."

And the young women who shall here find instruction and wisdom, what felicities do we not, in the rapidly widening career of usefulness opening out before them, invoke for them. Drinking deep of scholarship, as at a perennial fountain, in loving companionship with her bounteous aspects, may they be made strong with the thrilling transports of Learning, and confidently step forth upon the theater of action, fitted to be approved of God and adored of men, crowned with every womanly grace and virtue,

> "Priests, Sermons, Shrines."

ADDRESS

OF

SENATOR THOS. H. CARTER.

Mr. Chairman, Ladies and Gentlemen:

My neighbor, Senator Sanders, has well said that ill considered speech does not become the dignity of this occasion. The able, appropriate and scholarly addresses to which we have listened do credit to their authors and harmonize with the event we witness. While conscious that extemporaneous remarks may detract from, rather than add to the oratorical features of these exercises, I cannot forego the privilege accorded me of bearing witness as one of the audience to the thoughts and emotions born of our surroundings. The opening of this University will always be regarded as a conspicuous event in the history of Montana. A force has been set in operation in this presence to-day which is destined to be, and continue a potential factor in the struggle for higher and better civilization for unnumbered generations. To believe that this institution may survive the form of government under which it was brought into existence calls only for the exercise of faith in the love of a mother for a child unchangeable, even in the midst of political convulsions.

The State of Montana is entitled to a full measure of credit for bringing into form and active use this institution which may well be likened unto the keystone of an arch binding together and providing a logical climax for the public school system of the State. Although created by special legislative action, I cannot but regard the University as a part of our public schools, indeed, as the great high school of Montana. It is favored by a splendid endowment of land. A conservative view of the future gives to our University land grant a value far exceeding the original endowment of either Yale, Harvard, Princeton, Cornell or any of the older seats of learning to which our countrymen point with just pride. Let it ever be borne in mind that this great heritage came to us without price or petition from the hands of the National Government.

The atmosphere of these classic halls should ever be pervaded with the spirit of patriotism.

You, Mr. President, in speaking for the faculty have happily announced love of country as a sentiment to be constantly cherished and assiduously inculcated here. As a beautiful token of this living sentiment permit me to suggest that the starry emblem of national unity, the flag of the republic be always floated from the highest pinnacle on the building as a glorious witness of your patriotic purpose.

The action of this community to-day justifies the judgment of the legislature in locating this temple of learning at Missoula. You have shown your appreciation of the great importance and high mission of the institution placed under your immediate influence. The presence of so many farmers from distant homes on the Bitter Root and from remote parts of this large county, uniting with the citizens of Missoula to make this occasion duly imposing, serves another and a better purpose. This assemblage silently notifies all the people of Montana that their University is located in the midst of an appreciative, congenial and sympathetic community. The sons and daughters of Montana may be safely placed near the moral, social and intellectual life of a people who manifest such an active interest in the cause of liberal education. With a mission so lofty, a foundation so substantial and surroundings so auspicious, this institution will surely prove a credit to the present and a benediction to the future.

ADDRESS

OF

PRESIDENT JAMES REID.

Mr. Chairman, Ladies and Gentlemen:

It affords me great pleasure to bring you greetings from the College of Agriculture and Mechanic Arts. I am glad to be present and to have some part in this celebration of the opening of the Montana State University. This is indeed an auspicious occasion in the history of Missoula and the State of Montana, marking as it does, an important epoch in the progress of Higher Education.

As has been fitly said by a speaker who preceded me, civilization in its highest and best sense has to do not only with the material, but with the moral interests of men. It only realizes its goal in the development of a strong and noble citizenship. We may have a vast material development with its methods of railways, and telegraph and telephone systems, our ships may sail every sea and our flag may be seen floating from the topmasts of our merchant vessels in every harbor of the world, but all this is not in the truest and highest sense, civilization. If we would give it permanence and stability, we must develop citizens who are strong and noble and pure.

If our institutions of Higher Education would fulfill the end for which they are fostered and endorsed, they must regard the moral and spiritual nature of man. Only when all the powers are developed in harmony, is the man truly educated. Emerson speaks of the man who stands "four square to every wind that blows." I have no doubt he had in view the man who is so educated that he is completely master of himself, and has all his powers and faculties under control. Let us cherish the hope that this shall ever be the ideal of this institution whose opening we celebrate to-day. Making this your aim, we wish you God speed in your noble work.

ADDRESS

OF

PRESIDENT OSCAR J. CRAIG.

Mr. Chairman, Members of the Board of Education. Ladies and Gentlemen:—

On the first day of July I reached your beautiful University city, received the kind greetings of the Board of Trustees and the people, and at once entered on the duties of that office, now formally and publicly assumed.

These intervening weeks have been weeks of unremitting labor; planning the course of study, arranging the organization of the University, procuring material supplies, getting the building in order and projecting the University and its proposed work before our people of the commonwealth of Montana. I say our people, because I desire to claim at once all the privileges that attach to adoption, to be regarded as one of your number and as one who is interested in every cause and work that will tend to the development of this commonwealth. This institution within whose walls we gather to-day for the first time, is to be the State University of Montana. It is eminently proper that the State should take the lead in the establishment and endowment of educational institutions. The State is created for the good of the individuals composing it. Every influence that tends to elevate and ennoble the individual has a reflex influence that contributes strength, permanence, moral tone, and healthfulness to the commonwealth.

The highest ideal among the leading nations of antiquity was citizenship, but the individuality of the citizen was absorbed by the State. The citizen existed for the benefit of the State, not the State for the benefit of the citizen. This explains why so many centuries elapsed before the human race began to be elevated and to make substantial progress in civilization.

The interests of the individual were so merged into the demands of State that social and political rights were taken away from the people. The right of opinion and free speech had no existence and the ties of friendship and of kinship were of no importance when they came in contact with the prerogatives of State.

To-day we look at this question in a different light. We believe that the State is of use just as it advances the interests of the indivioual. We believe that any State which represses and restricts the free progress of its citizens is detrimental to their welfare. The great teacher pointed out this principle when he said that the "Sabbath is made for man and not man for the Sabbath." And so it is in the whole organization of government; men are not made for the good of institutions, but institutions whether human or divine are designed for the good of man. The mission of the State is not to minister to its own interests, but to protect the interests of the individuals who compose it, and as this principle is carried out will true civilization be advanced and humanity elevated and ennobled.

Every effort put forth by the state in the way of public education has a direct influence that tends to lessen the number of criminals, to do away with the pauper class, to abolish mendicancy and thereby to increase the prosperity of the state by decreasing the expenditure for jails, penitentiaries, benevolent institutions and reformatories. While education is not a panacea for all human ills still the statistics show that the greater number of those in our benevolent institutions as well as in our penal institutions are from the illiterate classes.

There is also the positive consideration that education increases the producing power of the individual, that the individual is able to become self supporting and a benefit to others just in proportion to his education. Add to these facts that other and greater positive consideration, that it is only by and through the education of his faculties that man can live up to the best that is in him and thus secure his highest good, and the argument is invincible that it is the first duty of a State to educate its people.

That governments are instituted for the good of the individuals governed is just as true in the educational world as it is in the political. There are departments in a university whose purpose is to facilitate research, but the course of study, the regulations, the general management are all for one purpose, the advancement of the individual student, and not for the benefit or aggrandizement of authority. In other words the purpose of the college is to benefit the student, and whatever tends to interfere with this result should be put aside both by the student and by the instructor.

In order that the greatest amount of good may be accomplished, there can be no contest or antagonism between teacher and taught, but on the contrary mutual respect, sympathy, and confidence. Without these the very best results can not be obtained. The best results can not be reached either in the class room or the laboratory if there is any feeling of restraint on the part of student or professor. The two must meet as friend meets friend, a common rule of right, a common sympathy and a common purpose. The relation of teacher and taught is one of mutual contract. It is this mutual friendship and co-operation that must give the greatest measure of success in every department of college life, whether in the laboratory, in the class room, or on the football ground.

I have not consulted my worthy colleagues in regard to the opinions set forth in this address, but I believe that I reflect the views that will direct the management of the Institution. An institution that has for its purpose the fitting of young men and young women for positions of honor, usefulness, and influence in the world. And to do this in such a way that when in future years they return and tread again these halls there will be nothing to regret and no vision of the past that will provoke a smile of pity for the lack of wisdom it may have involved.

Men and women who will recall their college days as the pleasantest of life; for in them there was not only pleasant companionship and the delights of intellectual achievement but in them also were fostered and developed those principles of character and conduct that have been paramount in protecting them from the evil of the world and guiding them to the achievement of success.

It should be a part of a liberal education to train to the use of right motives and to proper habits of self control. I have no sympathy whatever with that view which names as the three successive steps in a young man's life as "first a boy, then a student and afterwards a gentleman." It is closely allied to that other equally false view that places the terms tyrant and taskmaster as synonymous with teacher.

Somewhat different from these views but no better is that other notion which I regret to say obtains even in some schools on this side of the Atlantic. That it is necessary for the student to be polite and respectful and to observe certain rules because it is gentlemanly to do so. Thus putting the result above the principle that inspires it and making it of more importance to be gentlemanly than to be governed by right motives. Not a very correct code of morals, for all will certainly agree that the young man should "do right because it is right" and not for the sake of being a gentleman. These things that have been mentioned serve to hinder the administration of affairs on the basis of right and wrong and so some would bring in the element of expediency. This is an error for no amount of false reasoning on the part of students or on the part of the public should cause a doubtful policy to be used in the administration of affairs in an educational institution.

Perhaps one of the most important question of to-day is 'What is the best course of study?' What subjects are proper ones to best fit young men and young women for lives of contentment and usefulness?

In my own opinion there is a great deal more depends on the teacher than the course of study. It is not of so much moment what one studies whether it be Latin or whether it be Science. The important matter is what kind of a teacher gives the instruction.

The teacher who can awaken the students intellectual faculties to earnest effort and cause him to form habits of systematic thought and work is a successful one whether he be a Greek scholar or a Chemist.

Every man does not expect to remember the formulas of Chemistry, the theorems of Mathematics or even the aorist tenses of Greek verbs but a skilful teacher may make use of any one of these and obtain essentially the same result i. e. enthusiasm, proper habits of thought control, and proper methods of investigation.

It is eminently proper in this presence to discuss some of the distinctive aims and purposes of the University.

The University must cultivate intellectual freedom. Rational and conscious freedom are the highest ends that man can attain. The means used in attaining these ends must also be characterized by freedom. Freedom on the part of student as well as instructor. The student must learn to be free while traveling the path that leads to the highest good.

5—

It is in accordance with this principle that the student is able to direct his energies along the line of his greatest capabilities. Thus recognizing the individuality of the student. All minds are not cast in the same mold, although it took the world many centuries to make the discovery.

Some students will excel in the languages, some in the sciences others in the arts let each have freedom of choice and the greatest good will be attained.

The University must train to right habits of thinking and thought culture. The University is the conservator of the thought of the past, interpreting it and indicating its application to the needs of the present. The most of those who have a contempt for the past are among that class of reformers who believe the pulling down of existing structures to be a mark of progress, and when asked to begin the work of reconstruction have nothing more substantial to offer than airy abstractions and empty theories.

This is an age of material progress because it is an age of thought. Thought originates labor. Labor is the application of spirit to the material world. There is not an architectural structure or a mechanical contrivance that did not first exist in thought. The value of any material product of labor is in direct proportion to the amount of thought it contains.

History prevents us from being led astray by false conceptions and fallacious reasoning. It is the conservator of thought, for the final appeal is to experience. The people think and it is of the utmost importance that they be led to think aright, and be made secure against wild utopian theories and social romances that are still prevalent, but become less so as the benefits of a liberal education are disseminated. History teaches that we can reach nothing great or lasting but by addressing ourselves to the soul. If the sou decays there can no longer be great thoughts or grea actions. "Society lives by the spirit that inhabits it." It may for an instant submit to the empire of force, but in the long run it hearkens only to the voice of Justice. It was thus that the greatest resolution which history records, that of Christianity, was accomplished. It addressed itself only to the soul, but by changing the hearts of men it transformed society entirely and the material civilization of the world.

The University must fit men and women for their environment.

This is an age of activity and advancement. The one who succeeds will do so on account of his ability to enter into competition with others and win success by his own energy and acuteness. There is not a profession but has many followers. There is not a business but has many engaged in it. There is not an occapation that does not appear to be crowded. To insure success it is not enough that one is willing to work, to plan and to economize. Something more is rquired besides thrift and attention to business. One must be able to take advantage of every circumstance, and a circumstance is so constituted that to take advantage of it one must understand it. Things happen and afterwards we know their meaning. This will not do. We must be able to give the correct interpretation while the event is in progress. If we do not some one else will, and will also reap the benefit. Not only is it a requisite of success that we be able to interpret the meaning of facts as they occur, but we must know the probability of what is likely to occur. The man who succeeds must not only be equal to the emergency, but must be able to "create one where none exists."

Men are not so much the product of the times as the times are what men make them. It is not possible for one to isolate himself from the present and give his whole attention to his business, to the exclusion of surroundings. True, there are many who attempt to do this, but they never attain to more than a respectable mediocrity and live in a "fool's paradise" without knowing it. The successiul man of to-day is the wide-awake man. He not only knows his own business well, in fact a little better than any one else, but he knows something of life around him. It is this that has given us this peculiar age. Newspapers filled not only with current news, but with current knowledge. Magazines and periodicals with their rich stores of materials. Books full of reference to the present. History and economics are receiving more attention than ever before. Why? Because men want light on present problems. Some of the greatest problems of the age are social and political. And so the education of to-day must deal with the present. Because this is true we find a class of schools gaining in favor that not only furnish knowledge, but train their students in the application of it. Not the ancient history of the steam engine is demanded, but the ability to construct the most modern and improved form. Not the story of how Franklin discovered the identity of electricity and lightning, but the ability to design and construct the dynamo that will furnish the greatest amount of power and run the greatest number of lights at least expense. Not how the subject of alchemy has developed into modern chemistry, but how to conduct manufactures, prepare fertilizers and compound pharmaceutical mixtures with the least possible waste.

The University must tend to broader culture. Ignorance contracts, ignorance is intolerant. Ignorance is either rudely boastful or despondent varying always between these extremes. That one who knows himself best and has the best knowledge of humanity is the most sympathetic when sympathy is needed. That one who has opinions of his own, knows why he holds them, knows also the opinions of others and on what those opinions are founded is the most liberal and tolerant of the views of others. A knowledge of the past begets hopefulness for the future. Allow me to illustrate this thought by reference to our own political institututions.

The one who knows the least of our history and is least informed in regard to our political organization is the one who has the opinion that we are on the eve of destruction, but the one who knows our institutions and their history has confidence in the American people and confidence in our future prosperity.

Farther there is a personality of the individual which this broader culture develops. We come in contact with some men and afterward we are not able to find any impression they have made on us either for good or evil. We come in contact with others and ever after we remember and feel that we have gained something or have been made better by the contact. True culture will give true intellectual and moral worth. It will generate a force of character and a personality that will always exert a positive force for good.

The University is a place for preparation. No man has ever achieved anything great in this world without adequate preparation. There was but one Alexander and he had for his teacher the wisest man in the world—Aristotle. There was but one Hannibal and he commenced his military career at the age of 9. Columbus was no exception to this principle for he began a sea-faring life at the age of 14, having already distinguished himself in the University of Pavia by proficiency in his studies. For more than twenty years he is getting his practical training and making preparation all unconsciously for the great event. He is sometimes a sailor, sometimes a soldier, but wherever found is the same valiant and intrepid man. Before he made his proposition to the court of Portugal he was possessed of the best education the fifteenth century could furnish. He had possessed himself of the knowledge of the ancients. He was familiar with the accounts of Marco Polo, and had visited Iceland in order to find what knowledge might be gleaned regarding the voyages of the Northmen. Not only familiar with the thought of the age in which he lived, he was a recognized leader of thought when he went from Genoa to the court of Portugal. Before he started for the new world he had sailed a ship in every known sea. Of all the men of his age Columbus was the best prepared man to do the work which he did. The man who thoroughly prepares himself for his work is never a failure.

Columbus believed that by reaching the eastern shores of Asia a foothold might be obtained from which the banners of Christian Knights moving westward might yet wave over the Holy City of Jerusalem, and thus accomplish what the crusaders had in vain attempted. The result he did accomplish was much grander instead of gaining a tomb where a dead Christ had been buried he found a continent where the principles of a living Christianity have founded a civilization that has shed a beneficient influence on every nation under heaven.

America has been said to be a synonym for opportunity. America means more than this. America means freedom of conscience, a free church in a free state, that all honest labor is honorable,—that there is no aristocracy except the aristocracy of merit. That there is no nobility except the nobility of honest labor.

America will mean still more in that millennium that is to be, for in that golden future we shall see the "Brotherhood of Man" under the protection of the "Universal Fatherhood of God."

www.ingramcontent.com/pod-product-compliance
Lightning Source LLC
Chambersburg PA
CBHW020731100426
42735CB00038B/1879